The Seven Sacraments of Nicolas Poussin

The Seven Sacraments of Nicolas Poussin

NEIL BARTLETT

ROBIN WHITMORE

ARTANGEL 1998

PDB

It's never really ever quiet on the Whitechapel Road. When you come out of the tube station and wait to cross the road to the hospital you will be in the middle of a noisy, poor, ugly London night. When you get to the front door of the hospital, it will be just like it will always be when you arrive at a hospital; you'll need to go to the reception desk and ask where you should be going. There will be lots of other people there for lots of other reasons; they will be hurt or anxious or tired. You won't know any of them. They are all there for their different reasons.

You're lead down neon-lit corridors into what feels like the bowels of the hospital, the middle of it.

You go into the room where you've been told you should be.

The non-stop sound of a heartbeat.

A darkened and expectant space, after the brightly lit corridors of the hospital. Dark enough for the ushers to have to use torches.

As you take your seat you find a note taped onto your desk.

re. Bearstead Lecture Theatre/Poussin

Tonight will end with an invitation to leave this room and to be
escorted to the JOHN ELLIS LECTURE THEATRE for the final sequence of
this work. As an honoured guest, once there, you may stay and look
for as long, or as short, a while as you wish. The ushers have been
instructed not to interrupt or disturb you; nothing will happen to
formally announce the end of this evening - there will be no curtain
call. When you are ready to leave, you will be escorted back out of
the Hospital and to the street.

We would only ask that you end this night quietly.

Enter NB in a white doctor's coat with clipboard, pens. He briskly turns on the lights and washes his hands as if he has just completed his rounds.

...Thank you and good evening.

...With reference to the notes of which I trust you all have a copy on the desk in front of you.

He ensures that all the audience have read the notes, checks that all mobile phones and bleepers are turned off, as we are in the middle of a working hospital; puts on a clip mike. The lecture begins;

The classic account of the original display of the seven canvases we now know as THE SEVEN SACRAMENTS of Nicolas Poussin, 1594-1665, is that of Bellori, B-E-double L-O-R-I, Bellori. According to his *Lives of the Modern Painters*, Rome 1672, guests fortunate enough to have obtained an invitation to the Paris residence of Poussin's leading French patron, M. Paul Fréart de Chantelou, C-H-A-N-T-E-L-O-U, would have been invited to view the paintings only under very particular circumstances.

According to Bellori only the most distinguished of visitors would be invited to leave the dining room and visit the private apartments in which the pride of Chantelou's collection was hung. His account suggests that only one guest, on any one particular evening, would be accorded this much sought-after honour.

A single servant would light the chosen guest through the darkened

He dims the lights to near black-out

corridors of the house, he or she would then be seated and the room lit, Bellori significantly points out that this would all be accomplished in silence.

So, the room is dark, but there would be light enough for you to see.

The seven canvases were hung in a single room, which was apparently kept otherwise unfurnished. Each painting was of exactly the same dimensions, 117 by 178 centimetres, and each was kept concealed behind a curtain.

The Guest would indicate the canvas which he or she had chosen to view, the appropriate curtain would be drawn aside, and the servant would then of course quietly withdraw.

It was not possible to view more than one canvas at a time.

The great Italian Baroque sculptor Gianlorenzo Bernini, in his autobiographical account of his 1655 visit to Paris, describes how he became quite unaware of how long he was left to examine the paintings. He also mentions kneeling in front of one of them.

Presumably so as to scrutinise it more exactly.

When the Guest had looked at the painting for as long as desired, he or she would indicate that the curtain should be drawn again.

It is of course now standard practice that should the servant or any member of the nursing staff assess that the patient requires additional privacy during an examination then the curtain should be drawn *without* a request being made.

Thank you.

The seven canvases, now usually referred to by their collective title, were originally individually titled with reference to the liturgy rather than to their ostensible biblical subject matter. For instance, Poussin's 1647 depiction of the apparition of the Holy Spirit on the occasion of the baptism of Christ in the River Jordan as documented in the Gospel according to St. John, Chapter 1, verses 29-33, is properly designated **Baptism** - referring to the Sacrament itself rather than to the documented Biblical occasion of its first celebration. The implication of this title is that the canvas may be read as simultaneously representing both the baptism of Christ and any subsequent historical baptism. For instance yours.

Or for instance mine.

However, Poussin's composition of attendant figures in this first canvas does not feature either of my Grandmothers.

The other six canvases, in order, and with reference to the *Book of Common Prayer* of 1662, are:

two, **Confirmation**

three, **The Solemnization of Matrimony**

Penance

Ordination

Eucharist, also known of course as Communion;

and finally,

seven,

I should emphasise that this is not the order in which the canvases were painted, but the sequence in which they were intended to be viewed. When seen in this sequence the suite can be read as depicting seven precise moments, occurring in the appropriate chronological sequence, from a single day, with, for instance, **Baptism** taking place in the early morning, **Marriage** at High Noon, **Eucharist** later, **the same night** and then, finally…

It is appropriate to note here that statistically the most common time of death in terminally ill patients in this building is *indeed* the darkest and coldest hour of the night, which is most likely to occur at some point between three and six-thirty a.m.

Each of the seven scenes is illuminated by a different and realistically observed light-source.

I should point out for those of you who were hoping otherwise that there are no angels or supernatural interventions enlivening any of the seven scenes.

The first of the canvases was completed in 1644; Poussin's depiction of Extreme Unction, which is in fact the last of the Sacraments in the liturgy; and the sequence was completed, after five years of uninterrupted work, in 1648.

The subject matter of the series would of course have been familiar to the mid-seventeenth-century viewer. Poussin dressed his celebrants in the archaic costumes of the gospels and of first-century Rome; the ceremonies themselves would have been familiar in their contemporary form to anyone who saw these paintings.

This is also true of us.

Whilst we are unlikely, most of us, to have been members of the congregation at, for instance, an Ordination, or to have recently received the Sacrament of Penance on a weekly basis, few of us will not have attended, for instance, a baptism, or at least a wedding

Of some kind.

   At some time.

     For whatever reason.

We are perhaps one of the very last groups of people for whom this will be true.

In future we, just like everyone else, will have to bend down and read the labels under the paintings before we know what words the people in the painting are supposed to have just said, because we won't remember any of them from when we were children.

Our friends will have to follow the service in the little book they give out at funerals very carefully, because they won't remember any of those words from when they were children.

Our friends will have to be given a little xeroxed sheet which tells you what words you should use when the parent hands over their child,

or when you take hold of your partner's hand, in public,

or when you finally get the telephone call which says **you should come now, this is it. Don't drive too fast. No, she's not in any pain.**

When we look at old paintings we expect to be shown a picture of the way they did things at that time and in that place.
Not to be shown a picture of the way things might turn out tonight.
In this building.

I keep on remembering them wrong.

The words I mean.

And of course people say that's good, it's good to forget, you have to let go, you shouldn't try and remember things exactly as they were, you have to say goodbye.
But if these words are going to be forgotten, does it have to be me who is responsible for forgetting them?

In this our time the minds of men are so diverse that some think it a matter of great conscience to depart from a piece of the least of their Sacraments, Rites and Ceremonies, they be so addicted to their old customs and again on the other side, some be so new-fangled that they would innovate all things, and so despise the old, that nothing can like them but that is new. But consider; it is not necessary that traditions and ceremonies be in all places one, and utterly alike, for at all times they have been diverse, and may be changed. It hath been the wisdom of the Church ever since the first compiling of her Publick Liturgy to keep the mean between the two extremes, of too much stiffness in refusing, and of too much easiness in admitting any variations from it; therefore it is but reasonable that according to the various exigency of time and occasions such changes and alterations should be made therein,

yet so as that the body

He undresses and puts on a surgical gown.

the Body and Essentials of it
have still continued the same unto this day

for although the keeping or omitting of a ceremony in itself considered is but a small thing; yet the contemptuous breaking of it is no small offence.

Without some ceremonies it is not possible to keep any order.

And moreover, these be neither dark nor dumb ceremonies, but are here so set forth, that every man may understand what they do mean, and to what use they do serve

for the Sacraments were not ordained to be gazed upon merely, but that we should duly use them.

When the curtains are drawn aside from the paintings, no-one will ask you what you are feeling.

No member of the nursing staff will try and catch a glimpse of your face, or assume anything about what you are thinking.

When you indicate that the examination is complete,

the curtain will be drawn again
and it will be time for you to rejoin the rest of the party at dinner.

And the Servant, at that point, will say; Will you follow me now?

the lights dim

The first canvas depicts the Ministration of Publick Baptism; the familiar scene on the banks of the Jordan. In the centre, the first Baptism, that of Christ by St. John. St. John is the figure standing with his right hand extended. And assembled around him, the public. There are twenty figures in the composition; ten to the left of the Baptist and ten to the right, allowing Poussin a virtuoso display of classically-draped anatomies, particularly in the two figures immediately to the left of the Baptist, the two care assistants accompanying the next candidate being presented for Baptism.

Who of course feel like complete fools. At their time of life...

Being told that, as Godparents **they must faithfully fulfil their responsibilities both by the care of the child committed to their charge and by example of their own godly living.** And then being asked to answer the five questions,

and in public too,

the answers to the five questions being, for those of you not familiar with the form of the Sacrament, being;

Could you please speak up. **I renounce them all...;**

the second being, **All this I steadfastly believe;**

the third, **That is my desire;**

the fourth, **I will;**

and the last question of course is, **What is the name of this Child?**

RW affixes a hospital identification tag to NB's left wrist.

And the speaking of the name of the child is the precise moment when as the prayerbook has it, this particular body is **engrafted, incorporated, adopted, signed, received in the congregation**

welcomed
    and it is the moment when
    in the exact centre of the composition, an exact thing
    happens;
    from the raised right hand of the Baptist
    which divides the left side of the canvas from the right,
    and which is also aligned exactly with the waters of the Jordan,
    which divide the moment before
    from the moment to come
    from the raised right hand of the Baptist
    a single drop of water falls
    and in the moment that it falls
    the sun strikes the far side of the Jordan, and
    a dove appears, -

which could of course, depending upon your point of view, just as well be a trick of the morning light -

The light on the far side of Jordan is the same as the light over here, but better. More... golden.
It is very calm over there, almost empty, you can see almost for ever...
No-one in the painting is actually looking over Jordan, they
can't see what we can see -
Not the two care assistants, who feel like complete fools for
bringing him so early for his appointment, he's been waiting
there in that corridor for over two hours now -
Not the man kneeling here in a yellow robe with his back

turned
but although no one is looking over Jordan
it is always there; always.
Waiting.
Promised.
Always golden.
Always behind a curtain.

The last time I looked at this picture I realised that I had forgotten that peace was supposed to be even
a possibility.

And I had forgotten this group of four young men on the left hand of St. John
who are naked
and wet, because they've just been baptised, and there is a cold wind this morning, but somehow they
aren't cold at all.
One is drying his right arm
one bends his perfect back to dry his feet
one pulls on a blue sock
one turns and throws up his arms as he sees the sun come out over Jordan

and on their bodies
there are no scars. They have not been hurt,
They haven't steadfastly believed the wrong thing.
What they desire has left no marks on them.

Their skin is intact
People know their names and their date of birth without having to check who they are.

They're **welcome.**
And the man in the yellow robe, who is still dry, kneeling

here on the left hand of the Baptist, wants all this,
But he can't have it; not yet
Not for another six paintings, because
It isn't his turn yet.
And that is why he is looking so intently,
Waiting so patiently,
Directing his gaze so firmly at the right hand of St. John the Baptist.
That is why he has to be so sure that peace is a possibility
as at this very moment
a single drop of water
falls.

We hear the sound of a very young baby laughing.

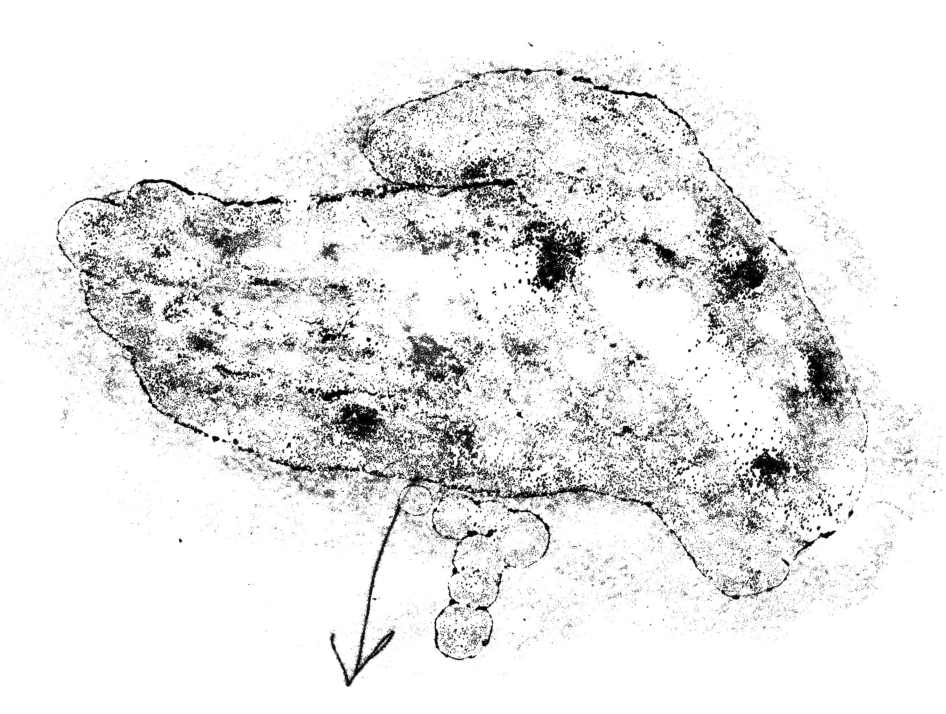

Three sanctuary lamps flicker.

The second Sacrament. The ceremony of Confirmation, in the absence of a Biblical precedent, is given an archaeologically exact setting by Poussin; a Roman catacomb, used as a refuge by the primitive Church. The darkened basement of a building, in the middle of the city.

The second canvas also features twenty-one figures in its composition, ten to the left and ten to the right.

The central figure, barely visible, is in this case a corpse, laid out and awaiting burial in one of the three sarcophagi which form the architectural background to the scene. None of the celebrants is apparently perturbed by the presence of the corpse; no one looks at it. Not even the children.

Which is funny, because anything on the TV with bodies involved I can't watch. I don't mean dying, it's anything with someone just lying there. Even people with their eyes closed, I go funny, I can't look.

And in the crematorium, when they draw that little curtain, at the end I find it such a relief.

In the wards here of course they draw the curtains,

When it happens.

In the mortuary here too they've got a curtain. In the room called the viewing room, where the relatives are shown the body after it has been laid out and covered. So that it looks whole again. They are ushered in, and the curtain is drawn aside, but behind the curtain is a pane of glass, 117 by 178 cm. This prevents them from touching it and trying to hold on to it, which they do sometimes. When they break down.

The sheet of glass needs cleaning frequently apparently; because people put their hands up against it.

When they have looked for as long as they need to, the curtain is drawn again.

I'm not sure whether the curtain makes it easier to forget what you have seen, or whether it makes you remember.

Still, you should be able to say whatever you have to say with a body in the room, shouldn't you?

And it's nice to imagine on these family occasions that the dead, in general, approve of the way we do things. And anyway, surely they like an occasion like this, a Confirmation, when there are lots of young people around.

So soon as children are come to a competent age, the age of discretion, **also Servants and Apprentices,** those of you that have them **upon the day appointed, all that are then to be confirmed, being placed, and all of them in order kneeling before the Bishop, he shall say -**

The order that you have to kneel in as you approach the Bishop to be confirmed, certainly the way that we did it in our church, is the order of age -

which is why the figure here in the right hand corner of the canvas is the youngest child, wearing a blue robe. He can't be more than, what, two, two and a half, in other words he's far too young to understand a single word of what is being said, and he's certainly far too young to be expected to keep quiet during such a lengthy service, he can't actually walk, this child, so of course he wants his mummy to pick him up, and he turns to her and she says SSSSHHH!!!!, look how your brother's doing it, see?
Above his mother's right hand, this child, the next in line, is seven. She hides under her mother's robe and says, it's not my turn yet.
Is it?

This boy is fourteen. Which is how old I was. He kneels in exactly the same place and in the same pose as the man who was waiting to be baptised in the first canvas. Now it is his turn to wear a yellow robe. Sometimes it is those younger than us who get the chance; that is true, sometimes.
He's doing it all very properly, this boy, he's learnt it all off by heart, he's looking very intently, he directs his gaze where he should, at the Bishop, but then at the very last minute he spoils it by turning round and saying to his mother
Am I doing it right?

Behind him, the next candidate is fifteen, a girl, she is very quiet, she's not kneeling, and her Mother has got her hand on her right shoulder, and she's actually pushing her daughter forward, saying go on it's your turn in a minute.
The boy in front of her, is five foot seven, tall for his age, he leans forward, because it is his turn next.
And in front of him, the boy whose turn it is, now, the oldest, the boy who has reached the age of -
RW You're still fourteen.
NB I learnt it all by heart?

22

RW **What is your name?**
Who gave you this name?
Dost thou think thou art bound to believe and to
do as they have promised for thee?

What meanest thou by this word Sacrament?
NB **A sacrament is the outward and visible sign -**
RW **Rehearse the articles of thy belief.**
What dost thou chiefly learn in the Articles of thy belief?
What is thy duty towards thy neighbour?
NB **My duty towards my neighbour is to love him.**
To hurt no body by word or deed; to be true and just in all my dealing; to bear no malice
nor hatred in my heart, to, to... -
RW Hands.
NB **- to keep my hands from picking and stealing, and my tongue from lying, and to keep my**
body - it was very hot the summer I was fourteen. I couldn't keep my shirt on, I used to get burnt all the
time. I wanted someone to... take it off me, I was... I used to get so...
... and it was always so very cool in the Church, dark -
and I learnt it all off by heart
and I promised
to keep my body, not to give it away to anybody even if they saw me with my shirt off
to keep it in temperance and soberness
Not to desire
to learn to **do my duty in that state in life unto which it shall please God to call me**
But it was *so* hot,
kneeling there, all of us in order
and eventually it was my turn, and the Bishop shall say,
My good child, know this, that thou art not able to do these things of thyself
And then you lean forward, **and he shall lay his hand upon the head of every one severally,**
saying

at this exact moment on the far left of the painting, behind the Bishop, there is an unlit taper. One of the alterboys is reaching up to light this taper from a burning candle on the alter - he steadies the candlestick with his other hand; he doesn't want to get burnt. One wick is burning,

and the other is bare,

and this is the exact moment when the flame will leap from one wick to another,

because I can walk now,

I am not too young to understand,

and I am not hiding in my mother's robe,

and I won't be quiet, because

I learn things by heart, it's the only way to learn them when

you're fourteen,

And it is your turn at last,

and at last you lean forward, and he…

places the thumb of his right hand exactly at the centre of your brow and you hear everyone,

you hear everyone there, severally, saying

O Lord
defend
this child

Dearly beloved, the third painting depicts the Sacrament of Marriage, and shows us **gathered together here in the sight of this congregation and in the face of** considerable public opposition **to join this man**
    and this woman
    in holy Matrimony
    which is an holy estate and is commended to be honourable among all men, and therefore is not by any to be enterprised, nor taken in hand, unadvisedly, lightly;

    to which the celebrant shall reply

    how very true.

There are twenty-four figures in this painting. The priest, in the centre, is in a yellow robe. There are ten guests with the groom, including a woman on the far right of the picture standing behind a pillar whose face you can't actually see, and ten with the bride, including that man standing right over there by the door, who I see has chosen to wear black, which I think is a very funny thing to wear to a wedding, he seems very unconvinced by the whole proceedings.
    And the twenty-fourth guest is me.
    And I'm here to provide the ring
    Because I'm not fourteen any longer
    And I choose to wear a ring.

And Poussin has placed it here so that the light from a window here on the left hand side of the painting falls exactly on it. Everyone is exactly placed. So that everyone can see. That's the point you see - you can't do this sort of thing in private.

I was sixteen the first time I saw two people actually doing it.

They made me an usher, I had to say to everyone,
Bride, or Groom?,

meaning are you with the Bride, in which case you have to sit on the left of the aisle, or are you with the Groom, in which case you have to join the figures on the right hand of the composition.

They ought to ask you that on the door of the club, really. You know, **Have you been here before, and are you Bride or Groom?** It's a very good question. Bride or groom, left or right, we haven't got all night dear, we close at two.

When I went to get the ring the woman in the shop was very brusque. Rather forward, actually. The thing is, according to the brochure, many people now find the traditional plain gold band frankly outmoded, and so, I thought, well, let's not be outmoded, let us not, tradition, ha! Well, it was bewildering. The choice I, mean. And there you are again you see, first of all you have to choose between *his* and *hers*. Which as several of you here tonight will I am quite sure be able to testify can be such a tricky choice to make, and especially *before* the wedding night, but choose you must, because apparently *hers* start at £750, *his* at £2100, because his are chunkier. Men generally prefer it chunkier, I was told. It was all I could do to silently nod my head in agreement.

We moved on to the next tray. "Modern simplicity".

Modern, yes.

Simple, I don't quite think so.

Something a little more showy?, she said.

So my friends are always telling me, I said.

White gold interlocking with matching gypsy-set cabuchon pink tourmaline was suggested.

Well someone had to speak up. Seems a little ostentatious, I said. Seems like someone feels the need to raise their voice, I said.

Newfangled, I said. What on earth would I be trying to prove?

Which is also a very good question.

Engraved she said?

Engraved, I said? Engraved, Tattooed, Scarred for life, I said.

Bruised.

On the surface or on the inside?

Quite, I said.

Time, date, names?

Very important, I said, So easily forgotten.

A few choice words?, she said.

How long have you got, I said.

Something basic, like "Everlasting Love" was suggested.

Something basic like full civil rights in the lifetime of this parliament was more what I had in mind not that I'm feeling particularly fucking civil I said and she said *are you taking the piss?*

No.

Though that is also quite a good question.

"Make of our hearts one heart"?, she said, which seemed to me to be pushing things a little too far, and it did raise the whole issue of his and hers again I felt, I mean its a lovely sentiment, lovely, in fact I think in a way those are some of the most effective lyrics Stephen ever wrote but look what happened to Maria and Tony, even death can't part us now... *in your dreams*. I mean you do find yourself thinking, don't you, are they the only two people in this entire cinema who've never heard of Romeo and Juliet, don't they know what happens? There is a place, somewhere absolutely, don't get me wrong, but really, George Chakiris maybe, Natalie Wood I don't think so -

she said could I just remind you that **no person whatsoever shall in any interludes, plays or by other open Words declare or speak any thing in Derogation, Depraving or Despising of the Form or Manner of the Sacraments.** *The Book of Common Prayer*, 1642, and I quote,

and I said *please*. Please don't tell me that you think that I'm joking. Not with the life I've lead.

Not with the life I'm planning on leading.

The life we're owed.

Hmmn, traditionalist, are we, she said? Assimilationist. Virtually Normal. Southwark Cathedral, that sort of thing. Something in Latin then, perhaps, she said.

Well, **To speak darkly is a kind of silence,** John Donne, 1627, I said, and I quote,

No, I said.

How about this one

It was my mother's,

It fits me, and inside it says

If any one here knows cause or just impediment why these two persons should not be joined together

let him now speak or else hereafter for ever hold his peace.

And then

The minister shall cause the Man with his right hand to take the Woman by the right hand and say after him

I take thee

and then the priest, taking the ring, shall deliver it unto the man, to put it upon the fourth finger of the woman's left hand

and the Man holding the ring there shall say

with this ring I thee wed

And the guests shall all lean forward, because this is the good bit,

the bit they came to see

and the woman behind the pillar, whose face we could not see, is in fact my grandmother, and I am so glad she's here to see this.

And the man in black watches, very intently, he stares - but not at the ring, at another man whose face says, I know,

I know

but people do say them, they say them all the time these words, and they let other people hear them say it,

and wouldn't you?

Can't you imagine what it's like to want to say those words,

even in secret, when it's late, and you're tired, and you can't even see his face, and it's filthy what you're doing, really filthy.

Or among the faithful, when of course no one in here minds if you kiss him, but you two mind how you go on the way home tonight.

Or right in the middle of town, in the middle of the afternoon, right in the midst of the congregation, when the priest shall then say -

Notice how in this composition the sun is about to shine down through an archway which is seen through the window which is directly above their hands as they are joined, and the window is garlanded

with flowers;
    take a step closer
    can everybody see
    as the sunlight comes through the arch and through the window and through the flowers and now exactly strikes the third finger of her left hand -
    Oh god I hate weddings.
    Someone always comes up to us and says, Hello, is this your friend?
    Well I can't have seen you since, well since you were kneeling down there in that yellow robe in the second painting. To have and to hold, it's such a lovely service, isn't it, with my body I thee worship, aren't they just the lucky couple, and look at you now, all these years later, still going to other people's weddings, I see you've chosen to wear black, funny thing to wear to a wedding, I see you've placed yourself as close to the door as you can but you haven't left, have you,
    and we can have no idea what he is thinking
    that man over there by the door.
    We should make no assumptions at all about what he is feeling as he listens very carefully, not unadvisedly, or lightly, as the priest says,

Those whom God hath joined together
Let no man
n o b o d y
Let no man put asunder

Don't even touch them.

As he slides the ring onto his finger a flash photograph is taken.

I will give thanks

With my whole heart

Secretly

Among the faithful

And in the congregation.

Psalm 111

Lovely the sun coming out like that. Needn't have used my flash I suppose really. Lovely. And lovely flowers I thought.

I do like a good photo.

And a video's not the same thing at all in my opinion, because with a video you can't put it in the book, can you? With all your other photos. Turn the pages over and see the people from one photo in another. There you are in your christening robe, there you are at Audrey's wedding and now look at you. And of course we all missed Grandma but there she is on the beach.

Nice to have something to look back on. Nice to have people with you.

On the wards here you'll often see that people have a photograph or two on the little bedside cabinet, well they can be very impersonal these wards can't they? And when somebody dies they say it's a good idea for the first *few* months to have a picture of them in every single room so that you can talk to them whenever you need to ask them a question or something. Also they can be watching you all the time, you don't have to worry about ever being out of their sight. It's nice to have one of them by the side of the bed at home.

Every night when I go to bed and as soon as I get up in the morning.

Funny though but anything on the TV with someone dying I can't watch. Can't watch it at all. Can't look at it.

I'm sorry.

I always cry at weddings. Actually I don't know about you but I cry a lot these days. I was watching this film this afternoon it was ridiculous I
oh

I'm sorry
I try and only do it when I'm on my own.
Never in public, I

oh I'm sorry

I try never to actually let myself go you see because once I started I'm afraid I'd never stop you see, I don't know -
oh I'm sorry. Excuse me.
Catch me walking down the street crying, I decided to give all that up almost nine years ago now. It was getting embarrassing. I used to be just walking down the street and then I'd -
Oh!

Sorry.
You see what I mean. Embarrassing.
Now I try and do it just when I'm indoors. Not in front of other people. Obviously I have to practise not making too much noise when I do it even then, I find having the television on helps and also a towel. Sort of on my face.
I mean you don't want people to pass the house and think oh dear what on earth is that woman crying for do you? I mean someone might come and knock on the door and ask you if you were - yes, fine, really, no, thank you... I'm sorry. Oh dear could you? I'm sorry, it's not as if I haven't practised believe you me. I don't want to upset anybody you see. I mean I wouldn't ever make a point of it. I wouldn't ever, I mean I wouldn't, I wouldn't ever walk into a room,
I wouldn't ever go into a dark room, because
All the men there would stop and turn and watch me doing it.
That's my absolute nightmare, I
Oh
Oh I want it to stop. This... sadness.

God I get myself in such a state. The third of the paintings, portraying the Sacrament of Penance, depicts the passage in the Gospel of St. Luke in which an unnamed woman, WHAT DID YOU JUST SAY? WHAT DID YOU CALL ME?, traditionally identified as Mary Magdalen, who is shown in this picture with her right shoulder exposed -

I'm sorry - I hadn't let myself go all evening
And I.
They were all bloody watching me
I went right up to him.
And I took hold of his foot in my right hand and I
I couldn't think about anything else, I
I was

... a woman who was a sinner,
when she knew Jesus sat at meat at the Pharisee's house, she stood at his feet behind him,
weeping, and began to wash his feet with her tears, and did wipe them with the hairs of her
head, and
kissed his feet, and anointed them. And when the Pharisee which had bidden him saw it, he
spake within himself, saying
This man, if he were a prophet, would have known who, and what manner of woman, this
is, that toucheth him; for she is a sinner.
And Jesus answering said unto him
Thou gavest me no water, but she hath washed my feet with tears
My head with oil thou didst not anoint; but this woman hath anointed my feet.
Thou gavest me no kiss, but this woman since the time I came in hath not ceased to kiss
my feet; let her alone. She hath done what she could
This she hath done shall be spoken of -
Wherever this gospel shall be preached, this that she hath done shall be spoken of for a
memorial of her.

And he said to the woman; Go,

go in peace.

Oh! I'm sorry - Peace. What's that then? Is
that what you call what I've never 'ad?
She had no bloody shame - she did it right there in front of all those men.
She bent over,

and I've done that.

She took 'is foot in her 'and -

I've done that

She opened her mouth... and

Pardon me... Really.

Go on *Pardon me.*

Pardon me for exposing the back of my neck to a stranger's gaze. Pardon me for saying you've got no idea how much I need this. Forgive me. Shut me up. Push me down with one hand on each shoulder, *make me.* Forgive me, for I have sinned right down in the very back of my throat, with three fingers down there, with the heel of a boot, with how bloody *thick* it is, with the whispers, the noise, the sounds I let out, I can't *believe* the words I say sometimes. Jesus.

Make me forget my own name.

Make me not care *Come on, make me.*

Make me do it again, and slower.

TURN THE LIGHT ON

Make me do it for money.

Make me do it in public places.

Make me do it in my parent's house.

Make me do it with your son.

Tell people all about me.

And then forgive me.

Flood me.

Dissolve me.

Wash me away;

Scatter me in drops, spill me, pour me out;

make me despair.

Wear me out, wring me out, begger me;

Wither me,

Spend me,

Waste, enervate, destroy and demolish me;

Make me despair;
And then forgive me.
For I acknowledge my faults.
Make me understand, make me a clean heart, *break me*
… and then forgive me.
Excuse me.
Pardon me.
Pardon?
Pardon me?
Catch me being one of those people who do it in public. Cry I mean. I can't stand that sort of thing.

The Magdalen is not depicted alone with Christ. Six of the other guests at the feast are staring at her
and four of them are pointing at her, they include a man having a drink who has no idea what she is talking
about and who obviously doesn't need forgiving, that's probably because he's got nothing to confess, two
men saying to each other did you see that,
                        did you see that -
                          and a man looking out of the picture straight at the viewer (the only one in
all the seven canvases who does that) raises his left eyebrow
and his left eyebrow says
I expect you all saw that
and at the very front of the picture
a young man who has seen and heard nothing kneels
and very
carefully
pours out a pitcher of wine
as she pours out her heart
without
spilling
a drop.

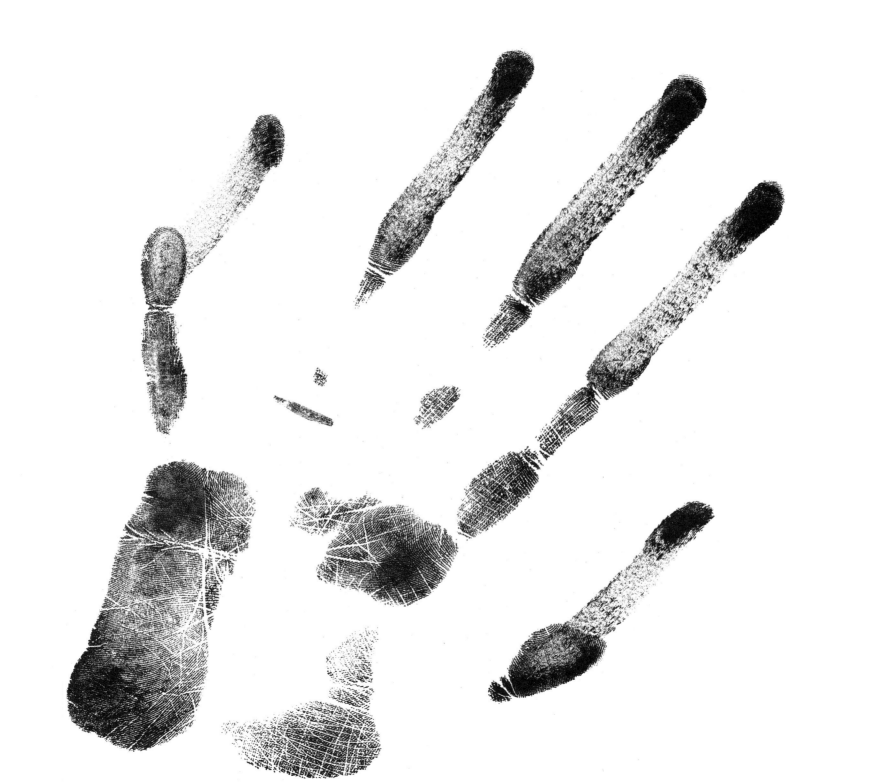

In the third painting the Bride has her hair covered and in the fourth the Magdalen lets her hair down. The Magdalen's skin is exposed and the Bride's is covered. One has a name and the other doesn't. Everyone is looking at them both, that's the same in both pictures, but don't tell me you haven't noticed the difference, I noticed it even when I was sixteen. The difference is the third finger of the right hand. Even if the ring has been taken off the X-ray will still reveal the characteristic callous just below the first joint on the third finger thus enabling us to distinguish between the accepted and the unacceptable.

There are no women at all in the next picture *Thank you*.

According to Bellori *Ordination* was painted in Rome, in seventy-seven days, in the summer of 1647. No guests were admitted or interruptions allowed by Poussin during this period. The biblical archetype of **The form and manner of the ordering of priests,** as the Anglican *Book of Common Prayer* styles it, is that recounted in the Gospel according to Saint Matthew Chapter 16, beginning at the sixteenth verse;
    And Jesus answered and said unto him, thou art Peter, and upon this rock I will build my church, and the gates of hell shall not prevail upon it. I will give unto thee the keys of the kingdom, and whatsoever thou shalt bind on earth shall be bound in heaven, and whatsoever thou shalt loose on earth shall be loosed in heaven. Heaven; Earth; Matthew, Bartholemew, Philip; James, wearing a yellow robe, Simon, Judas Iscariot; Thomas; Andrew; Thaddeus; James and his brother John; Peter, all of whom are apt and meet to exercise their ministry duly,
    and whom the Bishop shall commend to the prayers of the congregation, as followeth;
    that they be delivered from all blindness of heart, from pride vainglory and hypocrisy;
    that they be delivered from envy, hatred and malice, and all uncharitableness,
    from hardness of heart and from contempt;
    and they will, as our ministers
    strengthen such as do stand and raise up them that fall
    And then the Bishop shall say
    Take thou authority
    but none of them does.
    Because the fifth canvas does not show us the keys being taken; it shows us the moment when he says, go on, take them.

And no one there does,
which is odd
because someone has to.

Someone has to pick up the knife and perform the operation, it's not something you can do for yourself.

Someone has to make a diagnosis.

Someone signs the paper; someone has to.

Someone prepares the budget, after all, someone somewhere has to decide what things are worth these days.

Someone has to be prepared to explain, when the kids ask.

Someone has to pronounce the verdict - has to actually say the words.

Someone has to sign the paper and someone has to watch the door close.

Someone has to.

Someone must be the judge, if there is to be any judgement.

Someone has to say that if there is Justice there must also be Law.

Someone *has* to take the key, because someone has to turn it in the lock and shut people like that away
for ever and when they do you can't just ask to be excused, you can't just say you don't want to watch.

Someone has to be the keyholder. Why should it be someone else?

Are you scared?

Wouldn't you say that, at our time of life, that's frankly ridiculous.

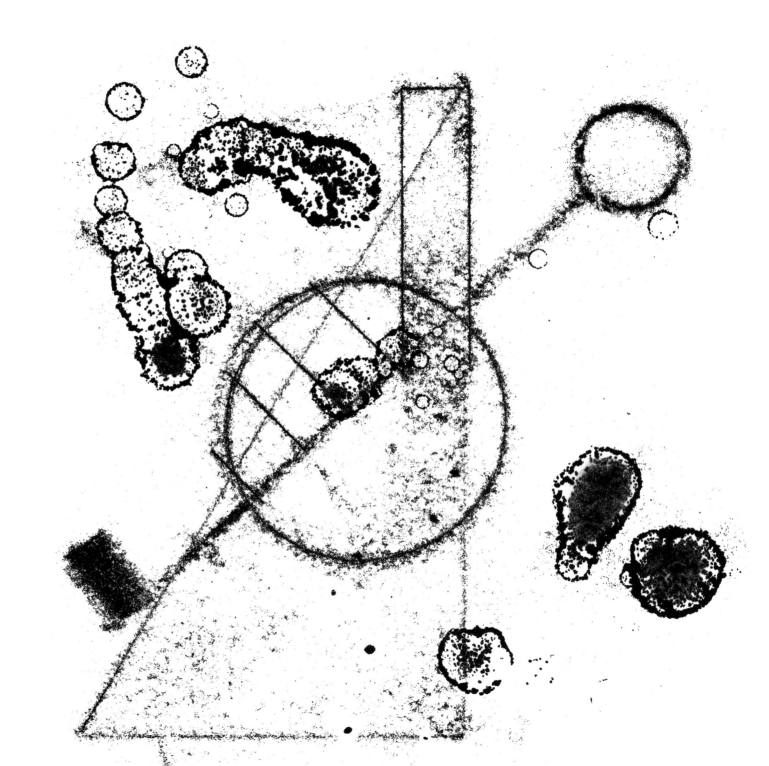

He takes his own pulse

Which arm would you like me to use? Just clench your fist for me a few times.

Sharp scratch. Press down hard for me.

He places a plaster over the mark the needle has left.

He takes pills.

He painfully takes off the surgical gown, his body visibly older and in pain, and lies down naked.

Lights Out Now Shall We?

You will have noticed, those of you that were brought up with these words as I was, that I keep on remembering them wrong. I have erred, and said things, like...

I've lost my place. I have left out the words which I ought to have said, and I've put in some of those that I ought not to have put in, and I just can't help it.

In the sixth painting there are the same thirteen men. But they are in a room now. The upper room. And it's later. And darker.

It is the night that he was betrayed.

In thy preparation to this holy and blessed Sacrament
Make this present day that day, this night, that same night, and consider what he did, and remember what you have done.
He spent the time till night in prayer
I dare scarce ask thee whither thou wentest or how thou disposed of thyself, when it grew dark, and after, last night.
About midnight he was taken and bound with a kiss
Art thou not too comfortable to him in that? Is that not too literally, too exactly thy case, at midnight to have been taken and bound with a kiss, and from thence
first to Annias
then to Caiaphas
then he was examined and buffetted and delivered over to those from whom he received derisions, and violences, the covering of his face, the spitting upon his face, the blasphemies of words and the smartness of blows, and then to the satisfaction of your fury, your haste for execution, to the scourging and the crowning of thorns and the judgement until there, hangs that body, embalmed in his own blood alive. There are those bowels of compassion, so manifested that you may see them through his wounds.

All of which is still to come.

At this exact moment, his body is not torn up like bread to be passed round, it is not broken, it hasn't been examined, it's not bleeding, there's no blood anywhere, and of all the one hundred and twenty one figures depicted in the seven canvases this is the one body which will never come into this building
this is the body that hangs there for ever
behind the curtain
and this is the body

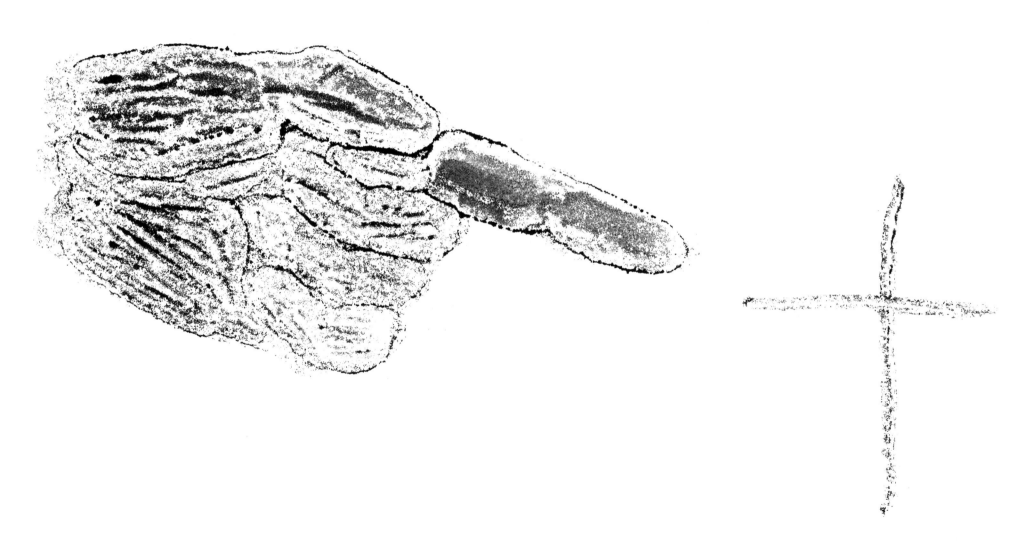

to the exact centre of which
with his right hand
not his left
he points.
Saying
This is my body
which is given for you

and at the exact moment that he says this

the Apostle to his right turns his head sharply, because he has seen that Judas is about to leave the room.

Judas stands where the guest in black stood at the wedding, right by the door, but he doesn't stay and watch.

He stands where the Magdalen stood, but he doesn't ask to be forgiven.

He is the only figure in all of the seven canvases who is shown actually moving; we see him walking out of the picture.

Because of this, we cannot see his face.

And because of that,

We can have no idea at all of what at this moment he is thinking.

We are all afraid to speak of death.

We are never thoroughly awake, but pass on with such dreams and imaginations as these; I may as well live, as another, and why should I die, rather than another? but awake, and tell me, who is this other that thou talkest of?

Is it someone else, somewhere in this building?

When Goliath had armed and fortified this body
And Jezabel had painted and perfumed this body
They said in their hearts, can these bodies die? -

And they are dead.

Look upon the water, and we are as that, and as that spilt upon the ground: Look to the earth, and we are not like that, but we are earth itself. At our tables we feed upon the dead, and in the temple we tread upon the dead, for when we meet in a Church, God hath made many echoes, many testimonies of our death, in the floor, and in the walls, and in the windows, and he only knows whether he will not make another testimony of our mortality, perhaps of the youngest among us here tonight before we part, and make the very place of burial, our deathbed. For indeed, no one knows their end, or the number of their days.

In the last painting, the seventh, there are again twelve figures gathered around a thirteenth. They are all there. The Quiet Girl from *Confirmation* is there, she's still fifteen. The Boy with the candle is there, he's kneeling with it now, because there's hardly space for everyone round the bed. The grandmother is there, and she's crying. The best friend, the man who threw up his arms when he saw the sun coming out over Jordan all those years ago is there, but he's not a year older, he throws up his arms again, he so longs to take the figure on the bed in his arms, but he knows you can't ever be sure if they are in pain or not, can you? Someone's brought the baby - the nurses must have said it would be alright to do that. Someone asks the doctor questions, as if that could help; and the doctor says the right things - because someone has to. One woman covers her face, she really doesn't want to upset anybody - and you can never be really sure if they can hear you or not can you? Another woman sits at the foot of the bed and weeps. She has no shame, and her shoulder is bare. The Nurse is clearly exhausted. It's been a long shift. It could be any time between three a.m. and six-thirty, she really has no idea. She is looking at the window and she is wondering if that is really the dawn that she can see.

The twelfth figure, right on the edge of the bed, the man in the yellow robe, is me. He is reaching out with his right hand, gently, and he is going to touch the back of the hand of the person on the bed. The first time that you see this painting you may think that there is so little air between his fingers and the dying hand that they are touching already. But in fact he is waiting for an exact moment,

The moment when the nurse says

yes I think this is it now

The moment when you lean forward and say

Go now.

It's alright, go.

Go

The moment when the breathing actually, finally, stops;

when the last breath isn't followed by a next one.

And at that moment, I promise you, no one will ask you what you are feeling.

Of course it may not actually happen like that,

it may be sudden, not everyone may be able to get there on time,

but that is the great virtue of this, the seventh painting, the last one, that whether you need to use it
to remember,
  or to use it to help you imagine
  what you just can't imagine,
  you do know that this has happened
  or will happen to everyone who has ever seen this picture.

  You do know that whenever you need it,
  it will always be there

  behind a curtain.

  Will you please all follow me now.

He leaves the room.

In a second room, which is quite silent, there is a hospital bed with the screens drawn back. He sits quietly beside the bed holding the right hand of the figure lying in it - except there is no figure there. Only a hollow in the pillow indicates its presence.

People watch for as long as they need to.

When the room empties you may become aware that you can just hear the first bird singing.

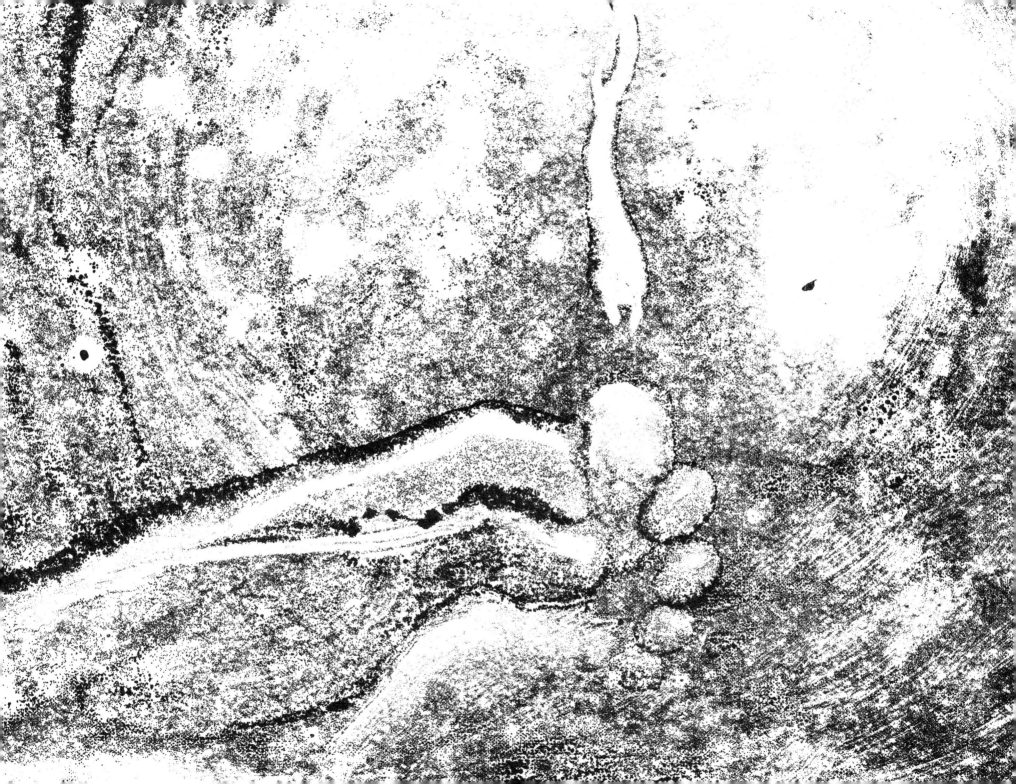

The Seven Sacraments of Nicolas Poussin was performed by Neil Bartlett in collaboration with Robin Whitmore at the Royal London Hospital, Whitechapel, London E1 from 1 - 7 July 1997.

The Seven Sacraments of Nicolas Poussin was commissioned by Artangel and produced in association with Gloria.

Design and binding by Book Works, London.
Monoprints and cover produced by Robin Whitmore at Book Works.
Text printed by Hand & Eye Letterpress and Book Works.

Artangel acknowledges the support of the Arts Council of England, the London Arts Board and the private patronage of The Company of Angels. Artangel Afterlives is supported by the National Lottery through the A4E scheme administered by the Arts Council of England.

ISBN 1 902201 04 3